# Coloring Book: Turtles
By K. Futterwacken



Published by Createspace 2018
Copyright © 2018 Kathryn Pierce
Author and Illustrator: K. Futterwacken (Kathryn Pierce)
ISBN-13: 978-1723307164
ISBN-10: 1723307165

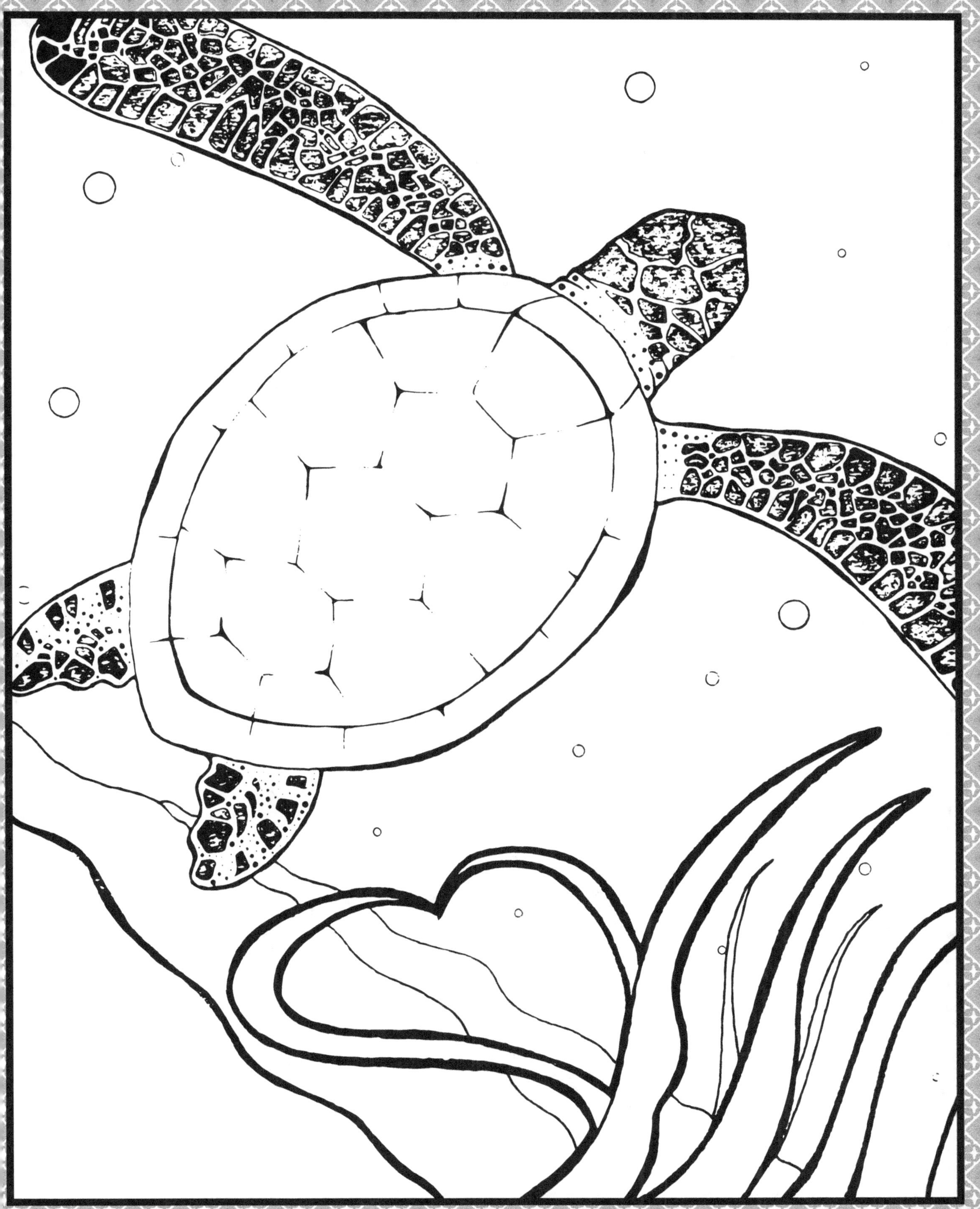

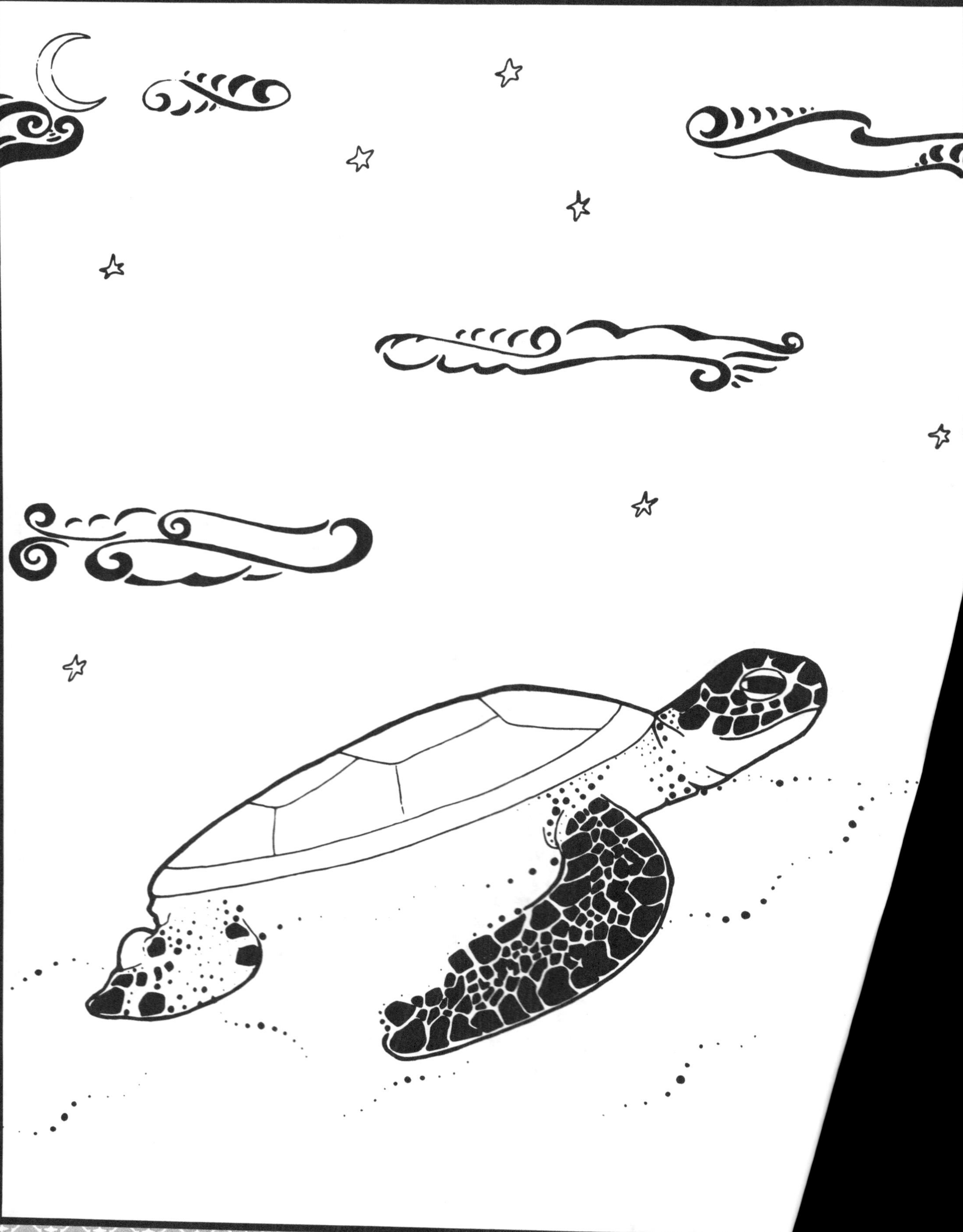

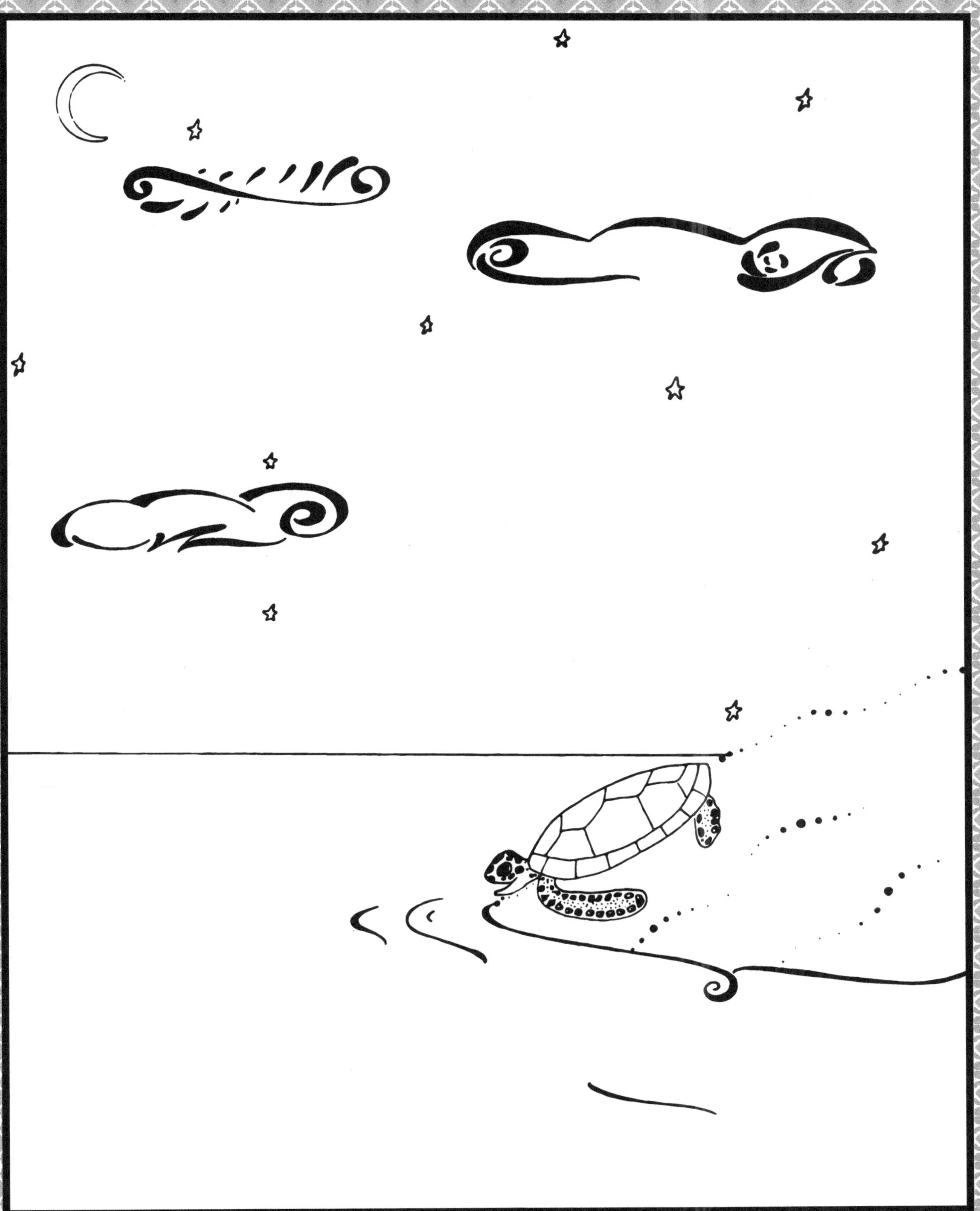

Social Media:

Handle: KFutterwacken
Facebook, Twitter, Instagram, Patreon


Email: kfutterwacken@gmail.com
Website: https://mischieviousfairie.wixsite.com/kfutterwacken
Soul Circus website: https://mischieviousfairie.wixsite.com/soul-circus